KNOCK-KNOCK!

WHO'S THERE?

IRISH.

IRISH WHO?

# IRISH YOU A HAPPY ST. PATRICK'S DAY!

How can you spot a jealous shamrock?

It will be green with envy!

Why are so many leprechauns florists?

They have green thumbs!

# What's big and purple and lies next to Ireland?

# Grape Britain!

*Find & colour in Grape Britain purple*

# Why do leprechauns hate running?

## They'd rather jig than jog!

DRAW A PICTURE OF A DANCING LEPRECHAUN

# How is a good friend like a four-leaf clover?

## They're hard to find!

A drawing of my best friend (dressed up as a leprechaun)
⬇     ⬇     ⬇

I'm lucky to have them as a freind because..........................
........................................................................................
........................................................................................
........................................................................................

What kind of bow can't be tied?

A rainbow!

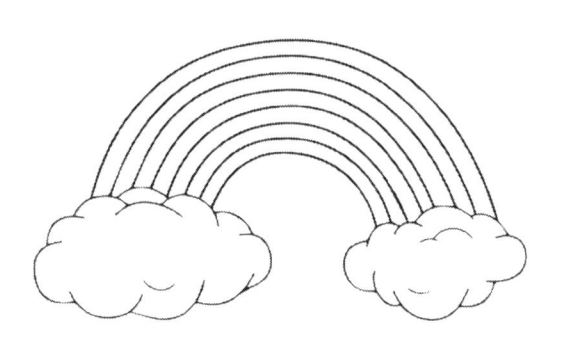

What would you get if you crossed a leprechaun with a Texan?

A pot of chili at the end of the rainbow!

Knock-knock! Who's there?

Warren.

Warren who?

Warren anything green for St. Patrick's Day?

My perfect St. Patricks day shirt

Why do leprechauns recycle?

They like to go green!

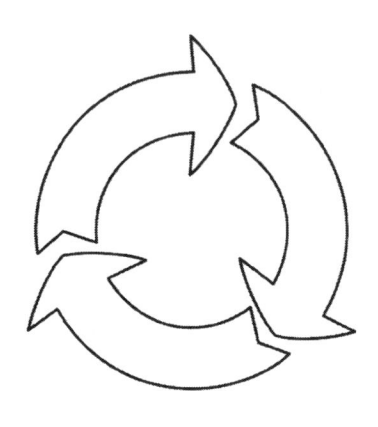

What's a leprechaun's favorite cereal?

Lucky charms!

What do you call a leprechaun who gets sent to jail?

A lepre-con!

••••••••••••••••••••••••••

Why did the leprechaun turn down a bowl of soup?

Because he already had a pot of gold!

# Why do people wear shamrocks on St. Patrick's Day?

## Regular rocks are too heavy

Why did the leprechaun walk out of the house?

He wanted to sit on the paddy-o!

What do leprechauns prefer dollar bills to coins?

Because they're green!

IF I HAD A POT OF GOLD I WOULD..........................

WHERE CAN YOU ALWAYS FIND GOLD?

IN THE DICTIONARY!

WHY DO FROGS LIKE ST. PATRICK'S DAY?

BECAUSE THEY'RE ALWAYS WEARING GREEN!

# What do you call a big Irish spider?

# Paddy long legs!

WHAT DID THE IRISH GHOST SAY TO THE OTHER IRISH GHOST?

TOP O' THE MOANING TO YOU!

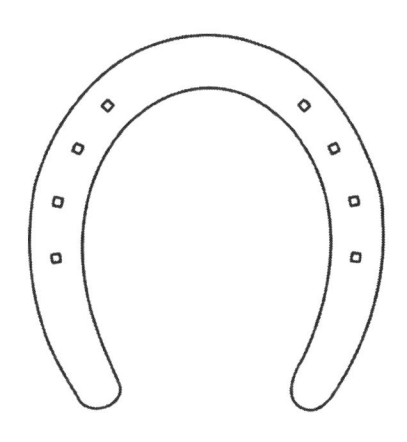

WHAT HAPPENS WHEN YOU FIND A HORSESHOE?

SOME HORSE IS BAREFOOT!

# IF A MAGICAL LEPRECHAUN GAVE YOU 3 WISHES, WHAT WOULD YOU WISH FOR?

☆

☆

☆

# WHAT IS A NUAHCERPEL?

LEPRECHAUN SPELLED BACKWARDS!

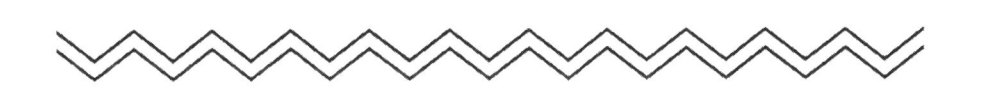

~~~~~~~~~~~~~~~~~~~~~~

WHAT POSITION DOES A LEPRECHAUN PLAY ON A BASEBALL TEAM?

SHORTSTOP!

Why can't Irish golfers ever end a game?

They refuse to leave the green.

How do you pay for soft drinks on St. Patrick's Day?

With soda bread.

WHAT JOB DOES A LEPRECHAUN HAVE AT A RESTAURANT?

A SHORT-ORDER COOK!

••••••••••••••••••••••••••••••••••••••••••••••••••••••••••••••••••

WHEN IS AN IRISH POTATO NOT AN IRISH POTATO?

WHEN HE IS A FRENCH FRY!

••••••••••••••••••••••••••••••••••••••••••••••••••••••••••••••••••

WHY WOULD YOU NEVER IRON A FOUR-LEAF CLOVER?

BECAUSE YOU SHOULDN'T PRESS YOUR LUCK!

Why are the Irish so concerned about global warming?

They're really into green living.

What did the baby find at the end of the rainbow?

A Potty Gold.

Who was St. Patrick's favorite super hero?

Green Lantern.

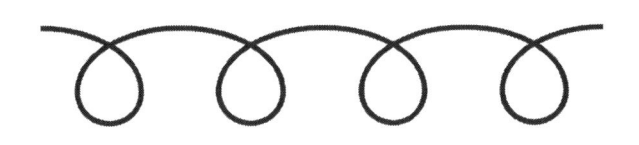

Why did Saint Patrick drive all the snakes out of Ireland?

Because he couldn't afford the train fare.

# What happens if you cross poison ivy with a four-leaf clover?

## You get a rash of good luck!

The luckiest thing that has ever happened to me......................................................................
..............................................................................
..............................................................................
..............................................................................
..............................................................................
..............................................................................
..............................................................................

WHAT DO YOU CALL A FAKE STONE IN IRELAND?

A SHAM-ROCK!

WHAT DO YOU CALL A CLUMSY IRISH DANCE?

A JIG MISTAKE!

Why can't you borrow money from a leprechaun?

They're always a little short.

~~~

How can you tell if a leprechaun likes your joke?

He's Dublin over with laughter!

What do leprechauns leave out on their lawn all summer?

Paddy O'Furniture

What do leprechauns love to barbecue?

Short ribs.

Knock, knock.
Who's there?
Don.
Don who?
Don be puttin' down the Irish.

---

What did the leprechaun
say on March 17?

I dunno

Irish you a Happy
St. Patrick's Day!

# Why did the leprechaun climb over the rainbow?

## To get to the other side!

What does Ireland have a lot of?

Irish people!

--------

What is long and green and only shows up once a year?

The St. Patrick's Day Parade

--------

Knock, knock.
Who's there?
Clover.
Clover who?
Clover here and I'll tell you.

> I met an Irish boy at the St. Patrick's Day party.

> Parent: Oh, really?

> Child: No, O'Reilly.

Knock, Knock
Who's there?
Erin.
Erin who?
Erin as fast as I could.

---

Knock Knock
Who's there?
Ireland. Ireland who?
Ire land you in time out so be nice.

# What kind of coin did the leprechaun put in the vending machine?

## A lepre-coin!

DESIGN A LEPRE-COIN

What did the leprechauns use to get to the moon?

A sham-rocket!

What would happen if you crossed St. Patrick's Day with Christmas?

You would get St. O'Claus!

Why did the leprechaun get the job as a secretary?

They were good at shorthand!

Knock, knock.
Who's there?
Irish stew.
Irish stew who?
Irish stew in the name of the law.

What did the Irish potato say to his sweetheart?

I only have eyes for you

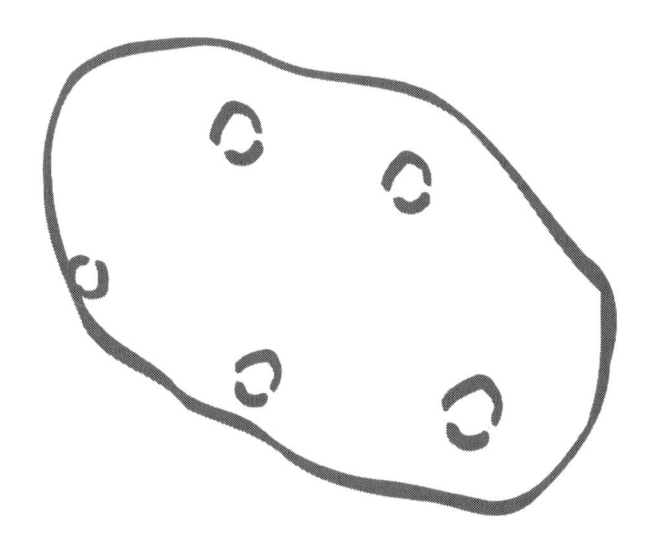

Why does the River Shannon have so much money in it?

Because it has 2 banks.

Why was St. Patrick given a desk job when he became a policeman?

He was too green to go out on patrol.

What did the Irish referee say when the soccer match ended?

Game clover.

What did the leprechaun call the happy man wearing green?

A Jolly Green Giant.

Why are leprechauns so hard to get along with?

They're very short-tempered.

Why did the leprechaun stand on the potato?

To stop himself from falling into the Irish stew.

How did the leprechaun beat everyone else to the pot of gold?

He took a short cut.

What musical instrument do show-off musicians play on St. Patrick's Day?

A: They play on their brag-pipes.

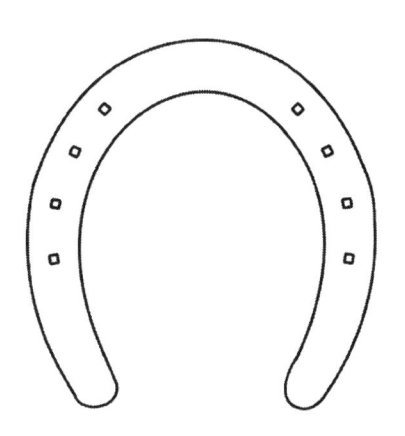

What do you call leprechauns who collect cans and plastic?

A: Wee-cyclers.

# What is a YADKCIRTAPTS?

St Patricks Day spelled backwards.

Knock, knock.
Who's there?
Pat.
Pat who?
Pat your coat on — let's go to the St. Patrick's Day parade.

What was St. Patrick's favorite kind of music?

Sham-rock and roll.

: What do you get when you cross a pillowcase with a stone?

A pilow sham rock

What did St. Patrick order to drink at the Chinese restaurant?

Green tea.

Why didn't St. Patrick visit the farmer to tell him a secret?

He wanted to avoid his shepherd spy. (Shepherd's pie)

Why was the leprechaun trying to find gamma rays?

He wanted to look like the Hulk.

What do Irishmen say when you tell them Bono is your favorite singer?

You too?

Why did the boy lock himself in his house on St. Patrick's Day?

He heard there might be leper cons running around.

What do sailors yell when they first see an Irish shoreline?

Ireland Ho!

# WORD SEARCH

```
I R E L A N D V M A S A K H M H W N
I S T J S A I N T K F H T Q A N H O
L R I L V G S L A H U V A U V W F D
J N I Z W F T G P Z Z G A M M N O X
R P W S L E P R E C H A U N R Z T D
A S A F H D A Z Z V U W A Y F O N X
I C P R S R I I R I O S U C G G C S
N Y O G A M C Z R B E E R G Z O R K
B G T U M D L U C K Y M A R C H L C
O G R E E N E V K I I I L B A U J D
W R C X J P A T R I C K X Z Q P Y X
C B W U I W L O Q Y R M I Z U R K V
```

BEER
GOLD
GREEN
IRELAND
IRISH
LEPRECHAUN
SHAMROCK

LUCKY
MARCH
PARADE
PATRICK
POT
RAINBOW
SAINT

WHAT WOULD YOU CALL AN 8 FOOT TALL LEPRECHAUN CARRYING A LARGE CLUB?

ANYTHING HE WANTS.

///////////////////////////////////////////////////////

WHY DID THE LEPRECHAUN WEAR RED SNEAKERS?

HIS GREEN ONES WERE IN THE WASH.

///////////////////////////////////////////////////////

WHAT DID THE LEPRECHAUN SAY TO THE ELF?

HOW'S THE WEATHER UP THERE.

Knock, knock.
Who's there?
Leper.
Leper who?
Leper con and I'm here to pinch you.

---

Knock, knock.
Who's there?
Rain.
Rain who?
Rainbow leads to a pot o' gold.

Are people jealous of the Irish?

Sure, some are green with envy.

////////////////////////////////////////////////////////////

Why did the leprechaun tenor stand on the chair?

So he could reach the high notes.

////////////////////////////////////////////////////////////

What would you get if you crossed a leprechaun with a yellow vegetable?

Lepre-corn.

# What do you call an Irishman who keeps bouncing off walls?

## Rick O'Shea.

////////////////////////////////////////////////////

# What would you get if you crossed Quasimodo with an Irish football player?

## The Halfback of Notre Dame.

*WORD SEARCH ANSWERS*

```
I R E L A N D . . . S . . .
I . . . S A I N T . . H . .
. R . . . . . . . . A . . .
. . I . . . . . . . . . M .
R P . S L E P R E C H A U N R . . .
A . A . H . . . . . . . . O . .
I . P R . . . . . . . . G . C .
N . O . A . . . B E E R . . O . K
B . T . . D L U C K Y M A R C H L .
O G R E E N E . . . . . . . . . D
W . . . . P A T R I C K . . . . .
```

# MY OWN ST PATRICKS DAY
# 🍀 JOKES & DRAWINGS 🍀

# MY OWN ST PATRICKS DAY
## 🍀 JOKES & DRAWINGS 🍀

# MY OWN ST PATRICKS DAY JOKES & DRAWINGS

# MY OWN ST PATRICKS DAY
## 🍀 JOKES & DRAWINGS 🍀

Made in the USA
Middletown, DE
11 March 2019